NETWORK MARKETING

SUCCESS BLUEPRINT

Go Pro in Network Marketing – Build Your Team,
Serve Others and Create the Life of Your Dreams

KELLY CRUZE

GET YOUR
FREE GIFT!

WAIT! – DO YOU LIKE FREE BOOKS?

My **FREE Gift** to You!! As a way to say **Thank You** for downloading my book, I'd like to offer you more **FREE BOOKS!** Each time we release a NEW book, we offer it first to a small number of people as a test - drive. Because of your commitment here in downloading my book, I'd love for you to be a part of this group. You can join easily here → http://www.kellycruze.com/

If you're interested in Entrepreneur, Self Help and Business books then you **MUST** signup for these **FREE BOOKS!** It's easy to join just by going to my website → http://www.kellycruze.com/

TABLE OF CONTENTS

SECTION 1
THE SUCCESSFUL NETWORK
MARKETER BLUEPRINT

CHAPTER ONE

INTRODUCTION TO NETWORK MARKETING

Congratulations! The very fact that you have downloaded this e-book and you have taken the initiative to consider a move into a Network Marketing opportunity speaks volumes about your motivation. And, if you are going to find success in Network Marketing, you will soon find that motivation is what you will need more of than anything!

In an effort to give you a "back stage pass" into what Network Marketing is all about, we have assembled input from a panel of TEN (10) Network Marketing professionals who are currently making their living as Independent Business Consultants. Their knowledge, experience and **Secret Tips** will provide the truth about what Network Marketing IS and what Network Marketing IS NOT. You will also learn what it will take to be successful in this field, should you choose to embark on this amazing Network Marketing journey. So let's get started because the sooner you come to the end of this e-book, the sooner you will know if Network Marketing is for you!

Network Marketing is definitely a relationship business that requires you to work with people. So, if you do not like interacting with human beings, you will want to evaluate that situation right away. To be a successful Network Marketer, you will have to continue to grow and perfect your skills of connecting with others. Verbal and non-verbal communication will be important to your success.

Why Network Marketing?

One word. Freedom. Now this word can mean a lot of different things to many different people but one of the greatest benefits to launching your career in Network Marketing will be freedom. To some the freedom is financial, for others it is the freedom to make their own schedule so they can travel, volunteer or raise their kids. For others, it is the freedom of not being locked in to the four walls of an office. Whatever freedom means to you, Network Marketing can most likely offer it to you.

Additionally, opportunities in Network Marketing provide a level playing field no matter what your education level, current income bracket or business experience. Our panel of Network Marketing professionals is as different in their backgrounds as are the products they represent.

This fact alone should get you pretty fired up and excited to know that it makes no difference whether or not you have a college degree, a GED, an MBA or if you are a single mother, a blue collar worker, someone looking for a career change or straight out of school with no work experience whatsoever.

You CAN be successful in Network Marketing and this e-book will tell you exactly what it takes to make Network Marketing a very lucrative career choice. But let's get VERY real; Network Marketing is not a money-for-nothing scenario. You will get out of it EXACTLY what you put into it so be aware that Network Marketing is not for the faint at heart nor is it for the lazy procrastinators looking for a quick buck.

There are many common denominators connecting successful Network Marketers but expecting something-for-nothing is not one of those common denominators. If you are looking for the "silver bullet" on how to make $10,000 a day without lifting a finger, you my friend have just wasted your time and money by downloading this e-book ... BUT it is only a waste if you stop reading right now. If you forge ahead, there is still hope. So here is the very first secret from our panel of experts:

SECRET TIP

In the early days,

you will "work" harder than you ever have before in your life.

Today you must commit to doing what others never will

so tomorrow you can do the things they never can.

Network Marketing IS NOT A SCAM nor a Pyramid Scheme

If you are considering starting your own Network Marketing business, you must learn what it IS and what it IS NOT. We will talk later about filling your own "belief bank" about Network Marketing to ensure when people question your motives, your product and your business model, you are educated and prepared to calmly and methodically explain what exactly you are doing. You MUST be prepared to use these opportunities to turn the cold call 'negative nellies' into hot prospects.

The very simple reason Network Marketing gets a bad wrap and is sometimes classified as a scam is because it is often compared to a Pyramid Scheme. Let's examine what exactly a Pyramid Scheme looks like so you understand the difference.

Many, many years ago before the time of the Internet, the "chain letter" existed. This was a letter that was mailed through the US Postal Service to 20 or so of your family and friends asking them to invest money based on the promise that other people will invest money and that it will be funneled back to them and they will get rich.

This 'chain letter' example is a very simplistic way of explaining the Pyramid Scheme. The point is there was no product exchanging hands. There was nothing more than a promise to "get-rich-quick." Money in exchange for nothing is always a red flag. And in your search for a Network Marketing opportunity, you must be able to spot the red flags so you do not find yourself in the middle of a Pyramid or a scam.

Understand that a Pyramid is strictly a shell game and has no basis as a legitimate business. Typically, there is no product involved at all, just money changing hands with the promise of a large return on "the investment." Modern-day pyramids may have a low-value product, but it's clearly there just to disguise the money game.

SECRET TIP

The most basic of red flags is that if it sounds too good to be true, it probably is. The second red flag is that if someone asks you to invest money, with the promise of a "guaranteed" large payout without ANY product or effort on your part ... RUN!

Pyramid Schemes are illegal and are built on taking advantage of people by promising something that will never be delivered. In order for a person to actually make money in a Pyramid Scheme, many other people must lose money. You can spot an illegal pyramid scheme because it awards payments to participants for bringing other participants into the scheme. Ask the question, "What product will I get for my money and what will I be selling to potential customers?"

Whereas a legitimate Network Marketing company pays compensation to its members based on the sale of product(s) to satisfy demand by end-users.

While you will find that many people can make substantial money through Network Marketing, the financial rewards will ALWAYS be the result of your own dedicated efforts in believing in a product, trusting the company you represent, building an organization of people underneath you (known also as your "downline") who sells real products they believe in and are passionate about.

In the Network Marketing business model, Independent Business Consultants do not receive compensation solely for recruiting other members into their downlines. Instead, in most cases, they become eligible for increased discounts and/or "commissions" only when the new members in their downline purchase products for consumption and/or for resale to other consumers.

Network marketing is not a get-rich-quick scheme. Of course some people do make large amounts of money very quickly. Many would say those people are lucky. But success in networking is not based on luck. (Unfortunately, money won't sprout wings and fly into your bank account no matter what someone has promised you.) Success in Network Marketing is based on following some very basic yet dynamic principles that will be outlined in the following chapters.

How the Industry can Make You Big Money

As you will learn from our panel of Network Marketing professionals, Network Marketing can lead to BIG MONEY and incentive TRIPS to amazing destinations! It can also provide you with substantial freedom and time to raise your kids, volunteer with your favorite local charity or church and actually sit down for dinner with your family.

In the traditional career model of trading your time for money, the above-mentioned activities are sometimes difficult. To make big pay, earn big titles with a corner office and continue to move up the corporate ladder, one must typically work long hours and spend countless nights and weekends away from home and family. With all that being said, your salary will be your salary whether you work 40 hours a week or 80 hours a week, your salary will remain the same.

However, Network Marketing puts you in control of what hours you work. How much money you make. And what your daily work life will look like. Take for example one of our panelists, Summer Davis, choosing to stay home and raise her two kids rather than having them in daycare for 12 hours a day. Summer made $18,000 dollars last month (more than she ever made as a real estate agent) working for Young Living. She made a calculated decision that someone else would not raise her children and being an Independent Business Consultant made decision possible.

Likewise, Jeannine Kulig Quigley who works for Arbonne makes more annually in the Network Marketing Business than she ever did as a teacher! Nicole Breger, who runs simultaneous campaigns for Herbalife and Seacret has traveled to many exciting destinations, while on pace for a six figure income in 2016.

Now do we have your attention?

So at this point, you are sitting on the edge of your seat wondering how you can be like Summer, Jeannine and Nicole? Don't worry. We are not going to hold anything back from you. We have included their roadmap to success in the chapters to come, along with other expert panelists who you have yet to meet.

CHAPTER TWO

WHY MANY ARE USING NETWORK MARKETING FOR RETIREMENT PLAN B

While the traditional job market remains stagnant and many traditional retirement plans have taken a nosedive or families and individuals have borrowed against their 401k plans, the direct-selling industry is booming. More than 15 million people now make a full or part-time living as independent representatives for Network Marketing companies.

It is probably safe to say that at some point in your adult life, you have been invited to participate in network marketing business opportunity. Maybe you were invited to a candle party or a kitchen appliance party or perhaps someone has discussed your health or weight loss goals with you. Maybe you have been hesitant to get involved because your gut is telling you Network

Marketing is a scam. While some opportunities that seem to good to be true probably are, the Network Marketing industry is exploding with opportunity and as a result, it is positioned to be a solution to many people's personal retirement/savings shortfalls.

So while many people enter in to Network Marketing to beef up or replenish their retirement plans, a vast majority now can see their Network Marketing venture as their "Plan A" for retirement.

For Alan Jones, who represents Nerium Skin Care International, his Network Marketing business originally was started as a "Plan B" to supplement his retirement so he could live comfortably into his golden years. However, it's been so successful that it has also helped elevate his current standard of living. Alan owns his own hair salon, which is his primary job. However, the Nerium Network Marketing opportunity is a perfect fit in his salon and increases his weekly income significantly.

With a reported three quarters of Americans having purchased products or services through the Network Marketing model last year, there are no signs of this model slowing down any time soon. It has proven to be a very lucrative business model for a wide variety of products and services ranging from Tupperware, make-up and weight loss solutions to a growing segment of health and wellness products, power tools, and home/personal safety products such as taser guns.

It is no wonder that many Network Marketing business owners who started as part-time consultants to merely supplement their full-time incomes and retirement plans have since left their full-time careers to give full attention to their Network Marketing efforts.

AdvoCare provides innovative nutritional, weight-management, sports performance and skin care products that sparked the interest of school teacher Jeremy Bowen. Teaching and coaching at one of the Nation's top ten schools, of course anything that could enhance the performance of his student athletes, as well as his own three children, is something he was willing to explore. Although initially, he admits, he thought it was too good to be true and considered it to be some sort of a pyramid scheme.

But the success and physical changes he was seeing occur in one of his friends on social media was just too amazing to ignore, so he began doing some of his own research and investigating. What he found was major endorsements of AdvoCare from NFL athletes as well as Olympians. Furthermore, he found there were no mandatory inventory shipments, order minimums or mandatory orders to get started. He tried the product in late 2012 and by spring of 2014 his life and his career and his retirement plan was changed forever. He retired from teaching and became a full-time Network Marketing professional earning up to $20,000 a month.

With the average American heading into the retirement years with less than $100,000 in retirement savings, it is easy to see why Network Marketing opportunities could be the saving grace for many who are not financially or emotionally prepared for retirement. Many people are beginning to face the reality that there is just not enough in savings to retire and relax as they get a little long in the tooth. Additionally, there is an entire generation of workers who are fed up in their current careers, frozen pay scales, corporate indifference and lack of connection in their job that Network Marketing is proving to be the greener grass on the other side of the fence.

Many of our Expert Network Marketing professionals started in Network Marketing part-time but have since left careers in teaching, real estate, technology, corporate America and many other paths, slowly transitioning into Network Marketing full time. When you find the right product and the right company, you could find a solution to your very own retirement shortfall or your unsatisfying career.

Ethical and long withstanding Network Marketing companies are successful, in part, because they help their Independent Business Consultants satisfy many needs beyond just the financial. Stay-at-home moms find adult connections and income that make them feel significant. Coupled with making new connections and finding a purpose outside of the children, gives most an opportunity to learn something new and making a difference in their personal life and in the lives of others. Many of the Network Marketers interviewed for this eBook confirmed that they focus on what they are doing for their customers and team members, and therefore have found success in many other ways besides a growing bank account and revived retirement accounts.

CHAPTER THREE

CHOOSING THE RIGHT COMPANY

Every single expert on our panel of Network Marketing professionals agreed on this very important point: Find your passion in the product and fulfilling the needs of people then the right company and the money will follow.

Not a single Network Marketing professional on our panel sought out "the right company" FIRST rather they fell in love with a product and upon further research found the company lined up with their needs, ethics and personal goals.

Elizabeth Hough, an Independent Beauty Consultant for Mary Kay has left her career as a Systems Administrator nearly five years ago. While she loved the Mary Kay products, that she describes as the number one skin care products in the industry, she really fell in love with the Mary Kay Philosophy of "God 1st,

Family 2nd, Business 3rd" that has been the foundation of Mary Kay for 51 years.

Before you even consider what company you want to work for, focus on a product or service that you can get passionate about! Once you find your passion, and you are ready to search for a company, here are some considerations when choosing a company:

- How long has the company been in business?

- How much money did the company earn last year?

- What are the available resources to learn and grow?

- Is there a solid and successful up line in place that will help mentor and encourage you?

- What is the initial start up costs or mandatory inventory requirements?

- Are their recruitment requirements and minimums?

- Do you need a sponsor to get started with the company?

- What are the commission payouts, promotion levels and trip destinations and rewards?

- How many total consultants are there and in what territories do they work?

While many will shy away from companies that are not well established or that require large inventory buy-ins, Nicole Breger, a representative for SEACRET, makes the point that if you are passionate about the product and there are no red flags to indicate a scam, she reminds people, "the bigger the risk is, the bigger the reward will be." Getting involved at the top of the up line in a younger, less established company, will leave room for quicker and more significant income opportunities. She suggested also paying attention to who it is, asking you to get involved. For her, it was a very successful network marketing professional from whom she had received previous offers for another company on which she passed. Missing the million-dollar boat last time, she was not about to miss the opportunity the second time around with Seacret, with products that are manufactured in Israel with supreme care, using the latest technology and best chemists.

Most importantly, you want to find a Network Marketing company that provides a serious business model for serious people who wants to succeed. Find a company that has a proven system of consistent success where the design, creation and expense the corporate team has gone through becomes a road map for your own success. Find the company that provides the simple, proven and duplicable system and you will find your six-figure opportunity.

Important Points from our Panel of Experts

Jeremy Bowen with Advocare Advises to **Follow Your Interests.**

As an advocate for childhood obesity and a high school coach and teacher, its nutrition and health products made sense to find his passion in Advocare products. "Promoting and educating prospects about a product or service that your passionate about is the key to your success, according to Bowen.

Summer Davis with Young Living Encourages You to **Explore the Company.**

Once you have found product(s) you are passionate about, search for information about that company. Once Davis discovered she was going to try essential oils to help with her health issues including extensive allergies and a long lasting cough, she researched which essential oil company would best fit her needs. Do they belong to any professional organizations? Are they debt free? How long have they been in business? How do other distributors feel about them? How about ex-distributors, why did they leave? What kinds of exclusions do their terms of service require? Are you allowed to be involved with more than one Network Marketing Company at the same time? What are the promotion and advertising limitations? What is the company mission? Who are the competitors and how does it products stack up in comparison?

Kyle Hooker with Origami Owl Recommends to Research the Program

Prior to starting with Origami Owl, Hooker was a 5th grade teacher for eight years. After having her second child in the summer of 2013 she and her husband decided it would be more cost effective for her to stay home with their two children. After a year of staying home, she was itching to have an outlet that would enable her to do something fun while bringing in extra income while providing adult interaction. A teacher friend of Hooker's was an independent designer with Origami Owl who hosted a Jewelry Bar (what Origami Owl calls a home party) for friends and family to present the new product and talk about her experience with the program and attending convention. Hooker always loved the products that Origami Owl offers so she started asking questions about the Origami Program. Find out how the program works. Do they require a minimum monthly purchase? Does this purchase requirement grow as you are building Network Marketing down lines? If the company uses points, how much money do you really have to spend? Is the price of the main product reasonable for reselling? Or is their "wholesale" price more than you would normally pay for comparable product retail?

Nicole Breger with Herbalife Encourages you to Understand the Compensation Plan

The compensation plan for the company you choose is very important when building Network Marketing down lines. Many network marketing compensation plans are complex so it is very important to ask questions and make sure you understand how much money you can potentially earn with the company. Ask if you need to enroll a certain number of distributors before you can earn commission. Also, find out if your commission grows as your team grows.

Jenni Walters with Rodan + Fields Reminds you to **take time to interview the up line**. Taking time to talk to her sponsor, as well as the up line provided Jenni with important information about this legacy company from the creators of Proactiv. She discovered it offers four main regimens to combat the four major signs of aging as well as tools for at-home use to speed and maximize personal results; they also offer other essential skincare items to achieve your best skin possible. After talking with people from the company, she deducted, "the opportunities you don't take are the ones that you end up regretting most." She also discovered that as an eighth year teaching, Rodan + Fields worked perfectly as a part-time career. While she was initially skeptical of network marketing, talking with the up line, she realized with no inventory, no mandatory parties, it just made sense. Jenni found comfort and credibility in finding her up line professional, trustworthy and credibly knowledgeable.

Jeannine Quigley with Arbonne Sampled the Product and Likewise Passes on Samples to Prospects

If you have not had a sample of the product or service, make sure that you take the time to do this before you join the program. The last thing you want is to find the perfect company for you and find out after joining that their product tastes terrible, or doesn't preform as promoted. If the person who is trying to recruit you is unwilling or unable to give (or sell) you a sample, find another sponsor.

SECTION 2
THE NUTS AND BOLTS OF THE SUCCESSFUL

Network Marketer

CHAPTER FOUR

COMMIT TO WINNING

Network Marketing really can be your opportunity of a lifetime. But you will get out of it exactly what you put in to it. If you want to succeed in a way that you never could have imagined, you are going to have to stop dreaming about what you want and get committed to making it happen.

Of course, as we already discussed, your commitment to winning starts with choosing the right product and the right company. Once you find your passion for a product, find the company that will be as committed to your success as you are:

1. What kind of training does the company provide?

2. What kind of testing is required?

3. Is there course work or online classes for product and personal development?

4. Are there quarterly or annual conferences?

Once you have found the company that is committed to helping you win, you have no excuse but to commit to winning. There is no alternative for you but to win. This is your shot. This is the opportunity you have been waiting for and you have the power and resources to create exactly the reality you want for yourself and/or your family.

You will win. Do you believe that? Then say it. Say it out loud. Write it down. Say in in the car. Repeat over and over again. I am a winner. I am awesome! I am committed to winning!

Don't think your thoughts and words matter when it comes to your commitment to winning? Well after you have found your passion for a product, picked the company that wants to see you and prepare you for success, NOTHING is more important than your thoughts, words and attitude when it comes to your commitment to winning.

Commit to a New Skill Set

You will not find success if you stay exactly where you are today. And nothing will impact your future growth and success more than coming to terms with the fact that you do NOT know enough. What you do know is in danger of becoming obsolete by tomorrow. The constant changes occurring in the marketplace, in technology, in marketing and business means you must commit to learning new skill sets in both personal and professional development. This is not optional. It is an urgent necessity for your success and survival.

Consider you are launching your Network Marketing business in the most competitive business environment the world has ever seen and the rapid pace of change is at an all time high. As a Network Marketer who is soon to be leading a team of your own, you must commit to a new skill set which includes personal growth, professional growth and changing leadership abilities.

Be honest with yourself - how much time to date have you spent on personal growth? Of course you are busy and now is not the time to make any excuses. What you need to do right now is give your current situation an honest evaluation.

As you launch your Network Marketing business, you will have more demands on your time than ever before. But, if you are not committed to learning new skills, building on your knowledge base, gaining new experiences, and all the while carefully scrutinizing the ways you have traditionally viewed and approached your work, your skill set will become obsolete. Your career and success path will stall before you even get started. So commit to winning by learning new skill sets by:

1. Take responsibility for your own growth.

Don't depend solely on company training programs to expand your knowledge base. Company provided programs will be incredibly valuable and access to such programs is a good sign that you are working at a forward-thinking company. However such training programs are not enough to help you reach your full potential.

It's also your responsibility to carve out the time to grow. You might need to get creative. Turn off the radio and pop in an audio book. Rather than listening to music while walking or running on the treadmill, listen to a podcast.

Whatever you need to do to make time for growth opportunities, do it. No excuses. Commit to becoming an avid reader and an eager learner; always seek new information and ways to improve.

2.   Make your own opportunities

Assuming responsibility for personal growth is not just about time, but also about finding and seizing opportunities as they arise.

An excellent example of this is an individual who, started out on the deep into a down line, only to work their way up to a level near the top of the organization earning top awards, trips and in some cases insurance and benefits.

3.   Seek a leader in your up line who will help you grow.

The fastest growth comes from coaching by an attentive manager in your up line. As you consider what product to represent and what company with which to work, look beyond the initial income potential. Consider how your sponsor might contribute to your personal growth and help you build your own team.

4. Learn from the leaders.

Not sure where to turn to start on your path to personal and professional development? Explore the topics, books, and podcasts from any of the following industry leaders:

- Brian Tracy

- Les Brown

- Zig Ziglar

- John Maxwell

- Ken Blanchard

- Joel Osteen

- Richard Fenton

- Jeffrey Gitomer

- David Schwartz

- Dale Carnegie

- W. Clement Stone

- Spencer Johnson

- Claude Bristol

- Og Mandino

- Napoleon Hill

- Tom Hopkins

CHAPTER FIVE

How to Find Prospects

The Proof is in the Pudding

Time and time again, our expert panelist of Network Marketing experts gave examples of a prospect SEEING the results of their product. Once prospects see the results of what has worked for you, other customers and team members, sales will come simply because the proof is in the pudding. This is where being very selective about the company you represent and the products you sell become very important.

Always Be Prospecting. Always.

Within reason. You still must be sure the audience with whom you prospect makes sense and is a good match for your product(s). The company with which you choose to work is more than likely going to have a great strategy for you to follow in terms of finding and presenting to prospects. If they don't, that might be a red flag that leads you to ask more questions to be sure the company is a right fit for you. For example, Nicole shared that the prospecting mantra for Seacret is simple: "Mud on Every Face."

The point is that everyone you meet or anyone you talk to is a prospect and the goal is to get the product on him or her so they can see "the proof in the pudding." It is a great strategy and very similar to many of the other prospecting strategies of other companies. Because any type of sales company – especially network marketing companies – is essentially a numbers game, the more people you talk to is going to increase your sales. Sure you will get more NO's, but you will get more prospects saying YES as well!

SECRET TIP

The rule in any sales position is to count

on numbers, not on people.

Prospecting continually assures you will always have a full funnel of prospects, more than you can possibly get to, therefore setting you up for success. If you are counting on a small number of "sure things" you will typically be disappointed, when a large percentage of the "sure things" fall through for one reason or another. Prospecting for new business aggressively assures that you will never have too many slow days in a row.

Referrals

The true way to really maximize every sale with a customer is to turn that one sale in to many more by gathering referrals. Many people do not gather referrals simply because they don't ASK for the referral. The strategy of asking for a referral will do one of two things:

1) It will get you more sales through the people your customer already knows might have some interest.

2) It will open up an opportunity to discuss the customer becoming part of the team.

Selling with Stories and Photographs of Success

When it comes to prospecting, one of your most valued tools in your arsenal will be stories and photographs. Stories stick in our head and photos are worth 1,000 words. Both give you instant credibility because it takes YOU out of the sales pitch. Stories and photos also stick in the heads of our prospects because stories and pictures give life and real meaning to your sales presentation by knocking down the wall of mistrust or disbelief.

The benefits of stories and photos are a product of the world we are living in today. Each and every one of us is drowning in the white noise of over stimulation and information overload. Genuine stories and photos help cut through all of the noise and gets prospects to pay attention while giving you an opportunity to teach someone about the benefits of your product(s). Sharing success stories and before and after photos are also very important to help overcome objections prospects might have without directly disagreeing with what they have said to you about your company or product. Stories and photos are non-threatening and non-argumentative methods of getting your point across without seeming argumentative.

Much of the information you will be armed with will come from your company and to a prospect, much of this statistical information will seem to abstract or logical. Stories and photos get to the heart of people and tap the emotional space where the majority of decision-making takes place. Real stories and photos are something prospects will remember long after they have forgotten statistics or facts.

The better you get at sharing success stories and the more before and after photos you have in your toolkit to represent each product you sell, the more products you will sell and the more team members you will recruit to your down line. Stories and photos are a very "non-sales" method to selling. Rather than spouting off facts about your product and company, you can tell a success story or show a photo of someone who purchased your product(s) and met their goals or needs. Draw the logical connection between your product and the benefit that a current customer experienced.

Talk to people in your up line or talk to current customers who have used your products. A good story or photo is going to be relevant and engaging so you are going to have to practice and research to be sure you are armed with at least one story for every product you sell. Think about your favorite relative, friend or teacher in high school. More than likely, the person you are thinking of was an engaging storyteller, able to grab your interest and leave you sitting on the edge of your seat for more! Humans have a natural reaction to turn off and mistrust sales people, but when you are just a regular person, telling a story of success, you are creating a platform of trust and credibility that even the toughest critic will have trouble tuning down.

Be specific with your stories; don't use generic, broad brushed statements without details. You need to engage people with your success stories and the way you will do this is to be specific by using a customer name, the issue they had, the goals they laid out for themselves and the result when one of your amazing products was used to reach the customers goal! Remember focus much of your attention on the person, not just the product you are trying to sell.

The enthusiasm that is build will go a very long way in selling products and recruiting team members. The psychological impact that stories and photos have on a prospects subconscious is priceless and something a scripted sales presentation just will not deliver. It is impossible for your own enthusiasm not to shine through while sharing a success story or showing a photo that highlights the good, positive proof of how well your product(s) work. True stories and before and after photos keep your belief bank filled as well, because nothing gives you more confidence and reassurance then when you see your products working and helping people!

Network Marketing is not about taking advantage of your friends and relatives. Sure, network marketing does include retailing to, and sponsoring people from, your "warm list" of prospects. Sharing the products, services and opportunity with people you know is still the basic foundation of the business. But today we see more successful Network Marketers using sophisticated marketing techniques such as the Internet, social media, conference calling and other long-distance sponsoring techniques to extend their network across the country.

Using Social Media and E-mail

Of course the majority of successful Network Marketers are using social media and E-mail as their main marketing tools. Most companies will also give you your own personalized landing page so you will have an online presence that is branded with your name and your identity. More than likely you will be able to set up your website with auto responders so when you capture leads, the auto responder can follow up with that person. As you will read in a later chapter, one of the greatest keys to success in this industry is follow-up. You would be shocked to know the number of potential leads and potential sales that go unmade due to lack of follow-up Automation on the Internet has allowed a much more consistent method of following up.

But, with all the benefits of technology in this day and age, do not make the mistake of throwing all phone and face-to-face interaction to the wayside.

Those who care and those who do not

Many of the Network Marketing experts who shared information about their down line team gave two answers when asked about the number of people in their down line. The first answer when asked about the number of people in their down line was the total number. For example, Jeremy Bowen with Advocare explained that there are more than 70 people total in his down line. However, the second number Jeremy gave was the total people in his down line that actually cared. That number was closer to 9.

Eventually, you will learn to stop trying to sponsor people who you know are not serious about the opportunity. Rather than E-mailing and Facebook messaging everyone under the sun, there will come a time when you will seek out the people who are more likely to care about the opportunity.

CHAPTER SIX

THE ART OF THE INVITATION

A successful Network Marketer learned a very valuable lesson the hard way. (she asked not to be named for this particular situation) After selling a single product to a customer, she made a decision that this customer would never be interested in more products, hosting an in-house presentation, let alone becoming part of her team to sell products herself. She took it upon herself to count someone out. Never had a conversation or asked any questions. She simply passed judgment, moved on and never extended an invite to get involved.

Then one day she was speaking with the direct manager in her up line about an eager new recruit that came to her after trying one of the products. This particular recruit was on-fire and passionate about growing a team. And who was this recruit? The very person she pre-judged and never invited to get involved or host an in-home presentation.

SECRET TIP

Never ever EVER pass judgment about who will be interested. Never ever count anybody out. After all, the worst thing they can say is "NO"

The company you choose will most likely offer spectacular training on how to invite people to home parties or to try your product. Use the training and do not try to recreate the wheel. The tactics your company shares with you are proven techniques, so do not think you are smarter than the system. You can certainly build on the foundation they offer, but do no start from square one and try to find a loophole in the system.

Keep these additional tips in mind to build on the system offered from your company:

1) Make your genuine focus is on people NOT product or money

2) Ask support from your up line. Get them involved and ask for their help.

3) Do not be a salesperson. Successful Network Marketers take on the role of teacher. Your job is to educate prospects on the benefits of how what you have will help them meet and exceed their personal goals.

4) Avoid giving prospects just enough information to let them make an **uninformed** decision. You should have a goal to set appointments for your prospects to see a full presentation so that they can make an **informed** decision. Go for the AIN. (An Informed No). Get an answer. Warm maybes are your enemy.

5) Use e-mail and mass social media invites as a last resort. These types of e-vites are very impersonal and rarely successful. Try to use traditional invites through mail, phone or in person as much as possible.

6) Continue to add prospects back to your FOLLOW UP list until they have experienced your full presentation.

7) Avoid saying things like, "I just recently started..." or "I just recently joined..." or, "I want to take you to an opportunity meeting."

8) Get serious about your recruiting strategy. Recruit above your expectations. You are building an executive team for your company. You want the most successful, financially ambitious people on your executive team. If you are presenting to people who are more successful in business that your are, inspire their ego by giving appreciation on their business experience then ask them to help you invest in a new business with which you are working.

9) Brainstorm names of people you know on a blank piece of paper. Write down any name that pops into your head. Do NOT judge and count anyone out.

10) Build partnerships with business owners that are a natural match for your products. For example, skin and nutrition products are a great match for a partnership with salon owners. Make an appointment to present to a salon owner and get them interested in your product. Imagine the reach of prospects tapping into the salon owner's client base.

11) Create a loyalty reward from interested prospects who bring a friend.

12) Figure out the stats. One successful Network Marketer has discovered they must touch a minimum of ten prospects per week, have two parties per month to meet his recruiting and sales goals.

13) Know you audience. Jeannine Quigley from Arbonne knows her prospect base responds better to handwritten, US mailed invitations. Whereas Summer Davis from Young Living has learned that her prospects respond well to evites sent out via social media.

Sample Scripts

Again, your company is certain to have scripts for you to use but here are some very simple standard script samples so you have an idea of what you should actually do and say in inviting people over a phone or in person:

Phone Invitation (Script)

You: Hi Sally, it's _____. I'm actually getting ready to run into a meeting, but I've been thinking about you for a couple of days and wanted to give you a quick call while I had you on my mind. Do you have a second?

Wait for Answer

You: I have an important XX that I need to talk to you about. When can we get together in the next day or two to chat for just a few minutes?

Wait for Answer

Great. I'll see you at 3pm. I want to introduce you to my business partner if he/she is available.

Call your Sponsor in your Up line and tell them the date and time of your agreed appointment. If they can't go, call somebody else in your Up line to assist you.

If the prospect is out of town, you can do this way in your phone conversation:

You: Hi Sally, it's _____. I'm actually getting ready to run into a meeting, but I've been thinking about you for a couple of days and wanted to give you a quick call while I had you on my mind. Do you have a second?

Wait for Answer

You: I have an important XX that I need to talk to you about. When can I call you back when you'll have about half an hour and can be by the Internet?

Wait for Answer

Great. I'll call up at 7:30pm.

If you are talking to a person in front of you, you can do this way in your conversation:

Hey Sally! I am so happy I bumped into you!

I've actually been thinking about you and have been meaning to give you a call.

I'm running late for an appointment right now, but I have some important XX that I need to talk to you about.

When can we get together in the next day or two?

Wait for Answer

Great, I'll see you at 9:00am. I want to introduce you to my business partner if he/she is available.

CHAPTER SEVEN

PRESENTING TO PROSPECTS

The 7-Step Prospecting Presentation Plan

1) Always be prospecting. Always.

2) Be Prepared. Always.

    a. Be very familiar with your products and company

    b. Be familiar with the competition and how the products are different

    c. If you were referred to this person, name drop early!

    d. Have a success story ready to share

    e. Be organized

3) Smile (and mean it)

    a. It is nearly impossible to come off fearful and smile at the same time

b. If you are genuine, and you better be if you want to be a successful network marketer, you will build trust more quickly with a smile.

4) Stick to the script

a. If your company has provided you with scripts to use, memorize them and make them your own so you do not sound like a robot. But stick to them because obviously the scripts are tested and true! Don't reinvent the wheel thinking your way will be better because it probably will not be better.

b. In your presentation, you need to show that your company produces a high quality product that will show results.

c. You need to get to the point quickly while presenting to prospects:

i. Build Interest

ii. Show that your product makes sense for their needs and goals

iii. Close the sale

d. If your company does not have scripts, ask why? This could be a red flag for an unorganized company. However, in some rare cases, there might be a good reason why scripts do not yet exist. Take the time to research and build your own scripts. Do not shoot from the hip or wing it, instead talk to your manager and others in your up line. Ask questions. Record them. Take notes. Their past success is how you will build your future success.

e. Practice the script in a mirror. You might feel a little silly but practicing in your mirror will reveal things about your verbal communication skills that you have never noticed. For instance, you might find you look way too serious and intense – stop that! Also, practicing in your mirror will get the marbles out of your mouth and get you well on your way to a smooth and genuine presentation.

5) Ask for the sale

a. If you are able to get through your presentation, get product on them or in them when appropriate, and learn about their needs and goals, you will usually sell a product. Once you get through your script, you should always ask for the sale when you have all of your product information presented. If you do not ask for the sale, nothing will happen and you will never know if you could have helped the prospect with a certain need or a goal. When you ask for the sale, you will get a YES, get a question or hear an objection that you will probably be able to overcome. Each of these situations brings you closer to another YES.

6) Stop Talking and LISTEN.

   a. You must train yourself to become an active listener, if you are not one already.

   b. This means listening more than you talk so you can better understand the needs and goals of your prospect.

   c. Listening is also very important to hear the YES from the prospect. Often times you might miss the sale because you have not actually heard the word YES come from the mouth of the prospect, but they are dropping other clues. Therefore, assume that every prospect is going to mean YES even if they do not say the word. After all, you have a great product that will help the prospect.

   d. Listen to get to the root of an objection, which means understanding what a prospect is thinking and why they are hesitant.

e.   Active listening is going to mean you have to ask good questions.

Selling Largest to Smallest

Assuming you have already identified a prospect who will be a good fit with the products you sell, its best to shoot for the moon in hopes you get the stars. Under no circumstance should you ever attempt to sell your product(s) to someone who doesn't need it, but if you chose the right company with outstanding products, this should never be an issue.

Because you are representing the most awesome of products for a very ethical company with fair price points and intelligent bundles, you will always want to be tactical about the order in which you offer your products to a prospect.

Usually, you should start from the high-dollar items and work your way down to the smaller, less expensive products. There are two main reasons why you want to do this:

1)   All customers will generally receive more value for their money in the higher priced packages

2)   You need to give them something to say NO to so they can then say YES

Letting Prospects Say No

A good rule of thumb in selling to prospects is always let them say no to something. It may sound a little odd to want to set yourself up to hear "no" but this practice can actually work to your benefit.

If the prospect passes on a premium product or package you are selling, keep stacking the value of meeting their long term goal and current need, that way if they already have a "no" on the table with you, they are usually psychologically prepared to say "yes" to something because they know you have their best interest in mind. You should make it a practice to always offer the top of the product line to purchase because this is the only way you will know for certain that you are not being self-limiting and underselling what the prospect might buy.

Upselling

Upselling is increasing the initial investment that the customer has agreed to spend. With a new customer, the starting point is usually the suggestion you made to help them fulfill a need or a goal with your product. With a returning customer, the starting point sale is probably just reordering the product they purchased from you last time.

Because your goal is to get to know the needs, goals and reason the customer is thinking about buying, the starting point sale should only be treated as the first product for the actual sale.

After you secure the minimum sale, you want to continue to conversation to gain a better understanding of the "Why" they purchased the product from you. Once you get to the why, you can better understand the actual need and the end goal. Certainly you have other products that will help your customer get on track to their end goal and one product alone will probably not meet all of their needs.

- Know as much as possible about what the initial interest in your product is for the customer

- Be able to make caring, well-informed suggestions relevant to the customer

- The key is making specific suggestions based on the knowledge you have about the customer and what the end goal is

Closing the Sale

Assuming you are representing the best company with the greatest products, you are going to have to ask for the sale and close the prospect. The process of converting the interest of a prospect to a closed sale is going to take work and skill. When you are in the "sales field" which is basically anywhere and everywhere you are, nothing is more gratifying then having a prospect buy product(s) from you to help them meet a specific personal need or goal. Closing is fun and rewarding! But contrary to what you might think, closing is not a natural skill for all. The vast majority of Network Marketers have had to learn to become great closers. Like anything else, developing your closing skills will require effort, time, and continual practice in your mirror, with your team and of course, with actual prospects. Your personal development in this area should be a particular goal over the remainder of in-office training, and in particular, during your first 60 days of launching your network marketing career.

What is the worst that can happen if you DO NOT ask for the sale to close the deal? NOTHING. And that is exactly the issue. Nothing will happen. Your prospects will not typically volunteer to buy products from you. That is why you need to close sales.

While your company will certainly arm you with strategies to close sales, here are the top ten ways to ask for the sale. Some will become more comfortable and natural for you the more you practice and put some of these to work for you:

1) Silence.

2) Assume the sale and offer options. "Now which product would you like, Product A which does this or Product B which will do that."

3) Suggest a product. "I think you should go ahead and try Product a first because we already discussed that it will help you with your goal."

4) Conclude and ask for the sale. "Do you have any more questions for me? (no) Great, Can I put you down for Product A?"

5) Suggest a product and share a success story. "Do you want to try the same product that Sally Smith took home? She had the same goal as you and had an amazing result in that she …"

6) Use a "yes" to get a decision. "Are you wanting to get healthy and lose weight this year?"

7) Suggest a priority. "I think we should first focus on issue A and then we can focus on issue B."

8) Ask a question you have already discussed to make the purchase common sense. "We have come to the conclusion that you definitely want to get rid of the brown spots on your skin. You have tried five over the counter products

already and wasted a lot of your time and money. We have established that this product has worked for many of my current customers. So do you want to start with the xx ounce size or the xxx ounce size?"

9) Have prospect make the choice. "So we have discussed three very specific needs and goals you have for yourself. Which of the three is most important to you to get started with?

10) Describe how the buying process works and how soon they will have product in hand to build excitement towards meeting their very specific need or goal.

CHAPTER EIGHT

THE FORTUNE IS IN THE FOLLOW-UP

The level of your success in Network Marketing will be in direct proportion to the follow-up you do with your prospects. If a conversation or sales call ends without a sale, do not be discouraged as it can take several follow ups to get a new prospect to buy. This can happen for any number of reasons, perhaps you have met the prospect at the very beginning of their thinking about a lifestyle or health change. Perhaps you caught the prospect at a time when they just did not have adequate time to listen to your sales presentation. Or perhaps the timing was off because the prospects kids are sick! You really might not know the reason you did not close the sale, but it will be your job to follow up until you get a YES or until you get a NO.

Now, there are those Network Marketers on our expert panel who admit do not do proper and aggressive follow up. And that is were we find the difference between those Network Marketers making an average of $50,000 to $80,000 and those making six figures! The fortune is really in the follow-up.

If You Do Not Get the "AIN", You Must Follow-Up

What does it mean to get the "AIN"? AIN = An Informed No. You can only get AN INFORMED NO after you have given your full presentation, talked about the prospects goals and needs and they truly understand what your product is all about. Many prospects will say NO without even understanding or knowing what they are rejecting simply because you caught them at a bad time. A prospect who does not know the benefits of your product or understand the value you bring to the table is NOT an AIN.

If you have a conversation with a prospect that does not result in a sale, this is not necessarily a NO. Never count a conversation as a NO just because you did not get a sale. Prospects will tell you NO very clearly if they do not want to hear from you again or if there is zero interest. You will learn that the majority of people who do not buy products from you did not actually tell you NO, rather they are people you never followed up with because you did not want to seem to pushy or too aggressive. Or you were fearful of getting a NO. Maybe you wanted to avoid more rejection. Or you were not organized enough to even remember that you were supposed to follow up!

Get an Organized Follow-Up System

You will be talking to hundreds and hundreds of people each month. If you think you are going to remember what the conversation was about, what they ask or if they ask you to follow up at a different time, you are sadly mistaken. There is no quicker way to defeat in Network Marketing than being disorganized.

The company for which you work will most likely have a follow up system to follow and if there is a system in place, use it. If there is not a follow up system in place, you are going to want to create one for yourself. It does not have to be complicated or fancy. Most of the expert panelists making a successful living in Network Marketing have a very simple and traditional follow up method that includes a daily calendar that has time slots for every day.

This is really all you need, when for example, Sally Smith asks you to follow up with her in two weeks, at 7 PM. You simply flip to that date in your calendar, and write Sally's name and phone number on the 7 PM line. Also, add some notes about what you discussed and what Sally's needs and goals are. Write as much detail down about each prospect and the conversation you had. You think you will remember. But you will not. Write everything down. Your bank account will thank you later. Go buy a calendar from your local office supply store as soon as you are done reading this book.

Of course you can put appointments in your iPhone, pad or laptop, but time and time again, people had horror stories of important information and appointments being lost by using technology. So it will serve you well to have a good old fashioned back up system.

How to Follow Up Effectively

Professional and timely follow-up calls or visits are very important to your path to a six-figure income in Network Marketing. The ideal prospect will buy from you on the first visit, but many prospects will not and your ability follow up with each of your prospects will mean the difference between being average and being a rock star. And let's face it; nobody wants to get into Network Marketing to be average. The discipline it takes to work a prospect until you get AN INFORMED NO or a sale is what will separate you from the average Network Marketers. You will either sell a lot of products or give up a ton of income based on your willingness to implement an organized and aggressive follow-up system. You must execute a follow-up system every single time. Do not go into a follow-up situation and shoot from the hip. If you do not follow-up with your prospects, it is going to cost you a TON of money.

Most of your follow-up visits will be made with prospects that might have brushed you off with some smoke-screen objections that only meant they did not have time to talk to you or maybe because they wanted to do a little more research or maybe they just were not ready to commit to the lifestyle change you discussed with them.

There are some key things you are going to want to learn to do when it comes to follow up properly:

1) Do NOT let too much time pass between your conversation with a prospect and your follow up. If too much time passes, you have created another cold-call situation and nothing is more painful than a cold-call. Following up within

72 hours is far less difficult because the prospect still has some warmth left from your initial conversation. Failure to follow up within 72 hours will result in a lot less sales.

2)   Never ask the prospect if they have had time to think about a product from you.   Here is the honest truth. The prospect probably did not give your conversation or your product presentation much thought after you got out of their face. What human nature will lead them to do if you do ask them this question is lie to you. They will feel guilty for not giving your product a second thought so they will tell you that YES, they did think about it and they have decided not to buy anything from you. Asking a prospect if they have given any thought to buying your product is a huge mistake and it will cost you a TON of money. So never, ever ask this question when you follow up with a prospect.

Follow-Up System

You are not always going to have the benefit of a face-to-face follow up situation. So you need to master a follow-up system that will work in-person, over the phone or in e-mail or social media scenarios.

1) Stay in Charge – You need to be in charge during every follow-up situation. Do NOT ask the prospect how they have been, if they have thought about your products or if they are ready to buy from you. You must be cool, calm, collected and genuine. Reintroduce yourself and the mention the products that you previously discussed with the prospect. Go right into the success you have had over the last 72 hours in helping others get on track with their goals and talk about how much product you have sold. Show that many other people trust what you are selling and are ready to change their life with your help. You MUST stay in charge for the first 25 seconds of talking (if verbally) and if in writing, you must make a confident case to show the success of what you have accomplished since last you spoke with this particular prospect.

2) Include a New Nugget – You have at your disposal a lot of great information, resources and stories of success. This information comes from your company, your up line, your own personal experience or via the research you have done. Bring to the table a success story or new information about a product you know will help the prospect meet their need or their goal.

3) Repeat the Highlights of your Presentation – You want to get the prospect excited again so hit on the highlights of your presentation that are relevant to this specific prospect. Focus on the points that are important to your prospect.

4) Ask for the Sale! Go for An Informed No! Close the sale!

CHAPTER NINE

TURNING PROSPECTS INTO DISTRIBUTORS OR CUSTOMERS

Imagine the response you would get if you were out on a very first date with someone and half way through your appetizer, you popped the question. Yes, THAT question! "Will you marry me?"

What do you think their response would be and what do you think they would think about the state of your mental health.

Much in the same way, you should never ask someone to become a distributor on your team during a first meeting. Remember, you want them to fall in love with the product and the results, benefits and amazing results that come from using the product(s) you are representing. So take your time and build the value. Remember, Network Marketing is all about running a marathon NOT a sprint.

Your first goal is going to be turning a prospect into a customer … and then a raving fan for your product(s).

Leave the customer satisfied and excited about their purchase and about the opportunity to become a distributor.

Recognize the Buying Signals

When you first start out on your Network Marketing business, your inexperience can potentially harm sales and prolong the selling process by missing unspoken buying signals that your prospect is putting out for you to catch. Hardly ever will someone say right away, "Yes, sign me up right now, let me get my checkbook." More often than not, their willingness to participate may not be so obvious. Rather you have to be on the look out for the willingness of the prospect to buy. You must actively be on the alert for buying signals.

A buying signal is an early alert that the prospect is willing to buy and ready to be closed. It is the link between your presentation and the close. The prospect might gesture, ask questions, or in some way communicate that there is an interest to buy the product you have been discussing. Your job is to recognize the buying signals and convert the signals to a sale. (Never should you push a product or sale on someone who does not need your product. But because you took your time to research the right company that has great products that will help everyone, this will not be an issue for you.)

While your company and the talented network marketers in your up line will be able to share specific buying signals with you, here is a snapshot of some common signals. These types of objections, questions and non-verbal actions must be considered buying signals showing that your prospect is interested in buying from you!

Product Questions:

- How long will it take to get my product once I order?

- How often will I need to buy new product?

- Will it come in the mail or will you deliver it by hand?

- How many customers use this?

- Do you have a sample I can try?

- What sizes are available?

Pricing Questions:

- How much is this product?

- Is there a cheaper size?

- If I buy two, is there a discount?

- Do you have any promotions or coupons?

Product Legitimacy Questions:

- Where are these products made?

- Where is your company located?

- How long have they been in business?

- How long have you been with the company?

Payment Questions:

- Can I write a check?

- Is full payment due today?

- Do you take credit cards?

- Do I pay taxes and shipping?

- Do I get any discount by ordering today?

- Can I order online?

Questions or Statements about competition?

- I currently use xx product without much success, why will this be different?

- Why does this cost more than that other companies products?

- I heard that xx company had better products then this product.

- I'm spending too much on my current products.

General Questions:

- Has this product worked for anyone else?

- Do I need to order today?

- How soon will I see results?

- Do you use this product?

- Is there a money-back guarantee?

Gestures or Actions:

- Prospect asks you to sit down or to get comfortable

- Prospect offers you something to drink

- Prospect pulls out current products being used

- Prospect takes your product or marketing material for closer review

- Prospect lets you complete 100% of your presentation

- Prospect smells or uses product sample and seems pleased

Obviously there are many other buying signals that cannot possibly be covered in one list. However, it is important to recognize these types of buying signals as only prospects with a significant interest in your product will ask these types of questions or make these actions or gestures. Pay attention for buying signals and be ready to make the next transition step towards your close!

CHAPTER TEN

GET NEW TEAM MEMBERS STARTED ON THE RIGHT PATH

As you get started on your Network Marketing career, pay special attention to the questions you have and the training process. Take notes and keep track of areas of strength in training but just as importantly, keep special notes on areas of which you needed additional follow up and clarification. Special attention given to your personal onboarding and training experience will be a key component of building a successful down line team.

As you build your down line team, there are several factors you must keep in mind to get new team members started on the right path. While the company you choose will certainly give you tremendous resources to successfully build your down line, the following are helpful tips gathered from our panel of expert Network Marketers.

1) Take time to develop the new members of your down line team.

You must duplicate yourself time and time again, so it is important to take the time with new people and walk them through the process to show them how you built your success. Do one-on-one training, as well as group training with your entire down line. As you are mentoring and couching, do not forget to stay active on your personal development as well. Your skills must continue to thrive and grow so you can be the best leader you can be for your team. Outside of training, one of the best things you can do to train your team is actually do the business, recruit new reps and obtain new customers together. This shows the new team member that the system works, products can be sold and new team can be recruited.

2) Show them the ropes of the business behind the business.

This is a business, and just like if you were the owner of a franchise or running a store, you need to have a business plan, a marketing plan, sales goals, a budget and of course, an accountant. You have all the same write-offs tax-wise that you have with running a store-front business, so it's very important to have your down line team research all the financial implications prior to making money from the Network Marketing opportunity. Prepare your team for how this career will affect them tax-wise. Discuss potential write-offs. There are also accountants who specialize in dealing with home-based businesses specifically in the Network Marketing industry.

3) Do not create a team of Orphans.

There's a term in the network marketing industry called "orphans"--when somebody is brought in and then the person who brought them in is just so busy bringing in other people that they don't spend the time to teach and train the new team members. You should be prepared to spend at least 15 to 30 days helping a new person come into the industry--training them, supporting them and holding their hand until they feel confident to be able to go off on their own. You really need to ask yourself, are you willing and able to do that? This is really about long-term relationship building. It's not about just bringing people into the business and just moving forward. It's about working with these people and helping them to develop relationships in order to set them up for success. If they struggle for too long, you will lose them and all the effort it took to recruit them to the team will be lost.

4) Tell them if they have a day job, not to leave it.... YET.

It is important as you recruit people into your down line that you encourage them to not leave their day job until the income meets or exceeds their current standard of living. It is your responsibility to explain a realistic timeframe as to when they should reach specific financial tiers. You also want them to spend a reasonable amount of time with the company so they trust the stability of the company, the product(s) and their up line.

5) Prepare them for the potential struggle.

Even if your new team member does everything you, your up line and all the online experts teach, there is the possibility that success will not come easily. Monitor their moral so you can work with them and get them back on track.

Encourage them to use the system, while inserting their own personality and creativity. Assuming you did your homework and you are representing a stellar company with awesome product(s) and top-notch training and sales aids, you will have a proven system for prospecting, sales scripts, recruiting, etc. However, it will be very important your team understands personal creativity, energy and personality is at the foundation of the system. You cannot fit a round peg into a square hole and likewise you cannot expect someone's natural talents to not be put to good use. Encourage them to use the scripts, know the system AND use it, but to find their own voice with their own personality.

CHAPTER ELEVEN

HOW TO PROMOTE YOUR PRODUCT(S) AND EVENTS

If you are told by your upline manager that events are optional and that success, sales and teams will all be built without events, stick that in your back pocket and plan on using events anyway. Remember, this is YOUR business and you have to build the skills of a business owner with a strategic marketing mindset.

SECRET TIP

Events. Drive. Business.

The term "event" can also mean meeting, home party, or conference. Also, keep in mind there are different types of events and meetings: one-on-one, two-on-one, small group, sponsored events, home meetings, home parties, local destination events, non-local destination events, regional events, hotel meetings and events. Each and every type of event can play a very important part of your success strategy.

You must find the way to get people to show up for your events. And that means you are going to have to be an active participant and never ever leave anything to chance. Events will be an important tactic in building your initial business and creating "raving fans" who will become your first of many team members in your downline.

Never leave anything to chance. One of our expert Network Marketing panelists, Jeannine, shared a recent experience that will serve as a valuable lesson. She was working with a prospect on hosting an in-home event at the prospects home. Typically, Jeannine is very active in the planning and preparation, down to sending out hand written invites. However, this particular prospect was very clear that her social circle best communicates using social media and that she had everything "under control" and promised a turn out of 8 or 9 at the home event. Jeannine, against her better judgment, let the prospect handle the invites and never was really given a firm number for people who would attend the home party. The night of the evening came ... and two people were there, the prospect and her mother. Always the professional, Jeannine continued on with the party and vowed never to not be an active participant in the planning and preparation again.

Use a mix of tactics when promoting for your event: phone calls, in person, hand written invitations, social media and day before and day of text reminders will go a very long way.

SECRET TIP

When people have committed to attending, ask them to bring something to the party to increase the chances of their keeping the commitment. Be prepared to reimburse them for the cost but also let them know how appreciative you are for their bringing ... the ice, or napkins, or a bag of chips, etc. Spread the assignments around and watch your attendance numbers increase!

Are there successful Network Marketers who do not use events? Of course, but it seems that it most likely the exception and not the rule. Therefore, as you are starting out and launching your Network Marketing career, you want to include event marketing as part of your strategic marketing plan to promote, sell and build relationships. The more successful events you host, the more $$ you will make and the more team members you will recruit.

SECRET TIP

Be committed to building an event culture

for yourself and your downline team.

Our panel of Network Marketing professionals shared endless ways to promote your products and promote your next event. Listed below is the compilation of all their ideas:

Social Media / Digital

- It goes without saying that Facebook is by far the most used tool. Some create private or secret groups.

- Do not forget creative uses of Twitter, LinkedIN, Instagram, Pinterest and even Snapchat

- Text Marketing

- Check your surrounding areas and product specific categories for online business directories, most of which are FREE, to ensure your business is listed were people can find you!

Traditional Methods

- Handwritten and mailed invitations

- Phone calls

- Face-to-Face invitations

Advertising / Media

- Small Home Town Newspapers – Ad space is priced reasonably and many have special nutrition sections or bridal registry sections. Ask for their editorial calendar so you can request your ad appear on that page to target the audience most likely to be interested in your product.

- Get a low cost outdoor banner printed with your business information on it. You can have these outdoor banners displayed at outdoor music/concert events, outdoor children's sporting events, outdoor adult sport events, outdoor neighborhood block parties, outdoor community events, carnivals, fairs, etc.

- Donate Product(s) to your local area Radio Station, they have numerous contests and they are always looking for sponsors. Your donation can be written off as a tax deduction plus you will get FREE Advertising & Business Exposure for your donation

- Community Clipper Coupon Packs & Sales Flyer Mailings. These days many communities have mailings that go out to every address in a community, contact them and see how you can participate and advertise your business.

- Local Television Stations are known to hold on-air contests & website contests for its audience. Contact your local television station to see if you can donate a prize or gift certificate to sponsor one of the contests. While there is a cost involved for you, the business exposure will be well worth the cost.

- Be sure to have your business listed in ALL the telephone book yellow pages or local buying guides in your community. Many also have a coupon section for additional exposure.

- Promote your business on affordable promotion items such as pens or pencils.

- Get a vehicle banner made for your automobile.

- Advertise your business in your local travel guide.

- Local City Maps is yet another location to advertise your business.

- Get your business info printed on balloons and then distribute them to local community centers, sporting events and other types of places where parents book their children's birthday parties. Balloons are also an affordable way to decorate and brand your tent / table at festivals and fairs.

- Work with other Independent Business Consultants in your community to team up on marketing efforts that make sense for a larger group. For example, sponsoring a local parade float or even a paid table at a business expo.

- Get T-shirts, polos, canvas tote bags or baseball hats printed with your business information on it (both front & back sides for t-shirts) and have your downline, friends, family and co-workers wear them to promote your brand in the community.

- Get a license plate made up for your vehicle. If you have your normal license plate on the back of your car, put your business named one on the front of the car. You can also get a vanity plate with your business name on it for about $20-$30 per plate, depending on your state.

- Wear a business nametag every time you go out into your community. Get a something printed on it such as: Ask me about (your company name) Product, I work from home, you can too, Earn some FREE when you party with me, Need more money?

- Local Area Magazines. Contact them about advertising but also find out if they need products for contests for their readers. Offer to donate a product or service for their contest and staff.

- Get business card magnets printed and hand them out everywhere you go!. Have your friends & family pass them out too. People are more likely to keep a magnetic business card compared to a regular one which gets shoved into a drawer or wallet. By having a magnetized card, your business is kept in front of the potential customer/client.

- Put an ad in the back of local high school yearbook.

- Put an ad for your business in local high school or college athletic sport program.

- Contact Local Churches & religious Groups and see if you can place an ad in their weekly church bulletins & program guides

- Do you have a local Community Play House or theater? Place an ad in the program.

- Co-Sponsor a Local Youth Athletic team. Baseball teams, softball teams, cheerleading squads, gymnastic squads and swim teams, etc. are always looking for sponsors. You business name and website will gain great exposure.

- Get a Yard Sign. If you have a home business consider getting a yard sign printed up and proudly display it in your front yard.

- Place an advertisement on the placemat of local restaurants

- Place an ad at the local bus stop bench or bus shed

- Monitor your local newspaper for Wedding, Engagement and New Baby Announcements! Make a list and then go to: www.searchbug.com

You can mail business information to each announcing your business, bridal gift registry, baby gift registry, etc.

- Stamp your business info to the outside of all outgoing postal mail. Include your business card on the inside. Do this for personal mail, business mail and for paying your bills.

- Ask about getting your info printed on golf tee's and golf balls & then donate them to a local golf course, mini golf course or fundraiser golf outings.

- FOAM DRINK COZIES, so people have your brand in hand while keeping their beverage can cold.

- Indoor or Outdoor Concert/Sports Arena. Numerous advertising and promotion opportunities. Look into signage or a promotional table opportunity.

- Children love stickers so buy a slew of stickers with your business name on them to hand out to kids in an effort to get your product(s) in front of the parents.

- Does your community print free Renters Guides, House Buying Guides or FREE Home Search publications? If so, contact any of these publications about placing your business advertisement.

- Local small town radio stations found on the AM frequency usually offer very low-cost local area advertising or are in need of local interview guests. This is a great way to get your business info out to those in your local community.

- Get your business info printed on inexpensive bookmarks then donate them to local area colleges, adult technical schools, book reading groups, libraries

- Draft a business press release and focus on the benefits of your product(s). Include some testimonial quotes from local customers. Include some research or stats to make it more newsworthy. Do not make it a sales piece if you hope to get coverage. Submit it to your local newspapers, local magazines, TV stations and radio stations. Offer to be a guest on one of their live or recorded shows.

- Consider getting some inexpensive mini desktop sized calendars printed with your business information and hand out to local office workplaces.

- Take the above idea a step further. Get your business info printed up on pencils, pens, mini note pads, tab stickers and so forth. Contact local office style businesses and donate a few "business" supplies to them!

- When you go to the doctors or dentists office you see a slew of these types of things from various companies all over the office, so you can do the same thing by donating them to office-style businesses.

- Get your business info printed on lanyards and distribute them to local office environments for employees to use to keep their keys on or give as freebies to your current established customers. If your product has a teen segment, consider giving to teens at colleges or high schools. (Teens have large disposable income and are a great target for your product)

Community Outreach and Memberships

- Many churches/schools hold a spring and Fall Fest so contact them about getting a table or a booth. Many times this will cost you under $15.00 to rent the space! Take products with you as well as fliers, catalogs, business cards etc. Do some sort of drawing too. Make up entry blanks that gather the customer's info so that you can initiate contact with them again within 7 days.

- Join your local area chamber of commerce since they are always holding local business events that you can participate in and help build your brand. This could also lead to speaking engagements.

- Contact your local area " Welcome to the Neighborhood Group." Ask them about including some free products and marketing material in their baskets/bags.

- Call your Chamber of Commerce, newspapers and colleges about Area Job Fairs. Get a booth or a table. A great recruiting opportunity as well as sales.

- Hotel or Motel lobbies, as well as Visitor Centers usually have a pamphlet wall or area for local area attractions.

- Check out your local area State Fairs & Community Carnivals and ask about getting a booth or table to distribute business information. If you products are has something to do on the spot, offer it for free… for example, a free facial every hour. People love to shop at Fairs & Carnivals and they are looking to spend money.

- Put your Business Knowledge to Work by offering to teach classes to adults.

  Examples: If you are with a kitchen/cooking company offer to teach adults to cook. They are always looking for fast & easy ways to prepare healthy meals.

  If you are a scrapbooking consultant, offer to teach a class to new moms on how to scrapbook new baby pages. If you are a Bath/Body/Spa consultant offer to teach pampering classes to women & moms. If you are a health and wellness consultant, this type of information could be priceless! You can find adult programs by contacting: Local Community Centers, Local Civic Groups and many High Schools & Community Colleges offer evening classes to adults. (continuing education). This generates leads & sales and only takes a short amount of time!

Gorilla Marketing Tactics

- Take a small zip close baggie (snack sizes work well) and include the following in it: Your Business Card, How to make $$ Flyer, a Piece of Candy such as hard candy or a lollipop, mini flyer of current host specials, discount coupon (optional) etc. Hand these out to the bank tellers, retail cashiers, in hotel lobbies, at your kids sport events, everywhere you go

- When you stay in hotels & motels, leave a catalog, a business card & discount coupon for the maid. Be creative when you leave tips for Hotel Maids, Waitresses, Waiters, Hair Dressers, etc. Don't just hand them your business card, make it memorable.

  Also, contact local area hotels, motels and bed & breakfast inns and ask them if you can do up a Lobby Basket and leave it in their Lobby. (make up little packs of info about your business & products and put them into the Lobby Basket for their patrons to take.)

- Contact local area bridal supply stores, bridal gown stores, caterers, tux rental centers, wedding dj's etc. Ask them if you can leave your business cards & fliers about the great product(s) from (Company Name) for them to give to their customers. Do not forget about sponsoring a table at the bridal shows that happen within a drivable distance from your home.

- Offer storeowners (focus on stores that make a good partnership with your product(s) a free gift or a personal discount for helping you spread the word about your business. Gyms, Salons, etc.

- Daycare Centers are excellent to contact and leave business cards and/or fliers print out a flyer of just a few items from our if you have a child or mom specific product. Attach your business card and a discount coupon.

- College Campuses, Dorms & Student Centers are a great place to prospect. Students are always looking to spend money and many college students are also looking for an extra income so target them to join your team as well. Student Centers also have local companies come in to set up information tables.

- Contact your local area hospitals and ask for Human Resources Department. Many hospitals hand out new parent goodie bags filled with products, samples and other items. It's FREE for you to add in your information!

- Contact your local medical offices, particularly Gynecology and OB Offices or even Pediatric Offices and inquire about leaving information with them for parents or children. Offer the gatekeeper some free product so they can sample what a great value added it will be for their patients.

- Contact local area car dealerships to hand out a small goodie bag for FREE to people who come in to take a free test drive.

- Target your local area gyms/health clubs or fitness centers. You can get a table space for $20 or less in most cases! Make sure you have products on display, plenty of catalogs, business cards and fliers. Focus on the target audience of the clients.

- Contact Companies in your area to see if you can come in and set up a table in the employee lounge or cafeteria for a employee shopping break.

- Does your local area cable company have a local information channel? Inquire about advertising, as these ads will reach thousands of potential buyers.

- Contact local small companies and shops to see if you can offer an exclusive discounts or freebie gift to their employees. Companies are always looking for a way to "treat" their employees to specials from the local surrounding community.

- Take your business on the road during nice weather. Contact local area parks & community centers to see what their schedule of events are and inquire about setting up a booth or table. This is a great way to network & market your business to those in your community.

- Contact local area businesses such as hair salons, massage parlors, boutiques, banks etc. and inquire about setting up a table for 1 week with 3 of your best selling products on it along with some catalogs, fliers, coupons and your business card. Offer the storeowner or manager a free gift for allowing you to do this. You can also offer to donate a prize for a raffle contest.

- Contact local area restaurants, bars and clubs and see about advertising on their paper beverage coasters.

- Attend Local Area holiday shopping events. Customers who are ready to spend holiday shopping money turn out for these events.

- Hold a local area community Block Party at your home or local community center. Families are always looking for something to do during the nice weather so be sure to set up a table with your product offerings or samples.

- When you give gifts to family, friends, neighbors, co-workers etc. make sure you give them gifts from your own company. This allows other people to see & touch your gift meaning FREE business exposure for you.

- Invite your spouse's co-workers over to your home for a party! Have a product display table set up and be ready to talk and sample your products.

- Do a neighborhood children's shopping party around Christmas or Mother's Day. Be price sensitive in these cases. Offer to wrap for free.

- Do a joint party with another consultant in a non-competing business. Partying with a friend is always fun and benefits the both of you. You can hold it at one hosts home, your home or at a local community center. Invite every one you know and have others help you spread the word. Hang up fliers at local centers & businesses too.

- Does your neighborhood hold local Meet & Greets? If so, make sure you attend those types of functions!

Get to know your fellow community members and network, network, network.

- Donate a Raffle Drawing Prize to a Schools, Non-Profit Group or Charity in your local community. They are always looking for prize donations for their charitable raffles. Make sure you get a receipt for tax purposes.

- Does your local area grocery store allow advertisers to place business ads on the back of their cash register receipts? If so, contact them about getting your business ad on there too. Offer a special discount or coupon.

- Research local baby expo's and baby events/contests to set up a booth or table with your business info. These events are always very popular and a great way for you to reach new customers.

- Contact your local Fire & Ambulance companies and see if you can set up a table at their next BBQ or fundraiser event.

- Contact local Assisted Living Centers for Senior Citizens (this is different then a nursing home) and offer a shopping opportunity to their residents.

Seniors cannot get out as often so they appreciate being able to shop from home.

- Investigate local concerts in the park and events. These are a great opportunity to advertise or set up an information table.

- Make up candy packs with your business info attached to them and hand out to the Halloween Trick or Treat parents while they are walking their kids around the neighborhood.

- Exchange Business Cards, Fliers or Coupons with another Home Party Consultant in a NON-Competing Business and place her filler in your bags & outgoing packages & have her do the same for you. For example, maybe she does health and wellness and you do skin care, a perfect combination.

- The PUBLIC Library is a great place for your local advertisement, catalogs and business cards.

- Print handbills and get permission from local shopping centers to see if you can leave them on car windshields. Offering the decision makers FREE sample products goes a long way in getting the green light.

- Ask the local ice cream man who drives around in his ice cream truck about passing out flyers or letting you add a logo onto his truck via a vinyl cling logo banner. A great opportunity for branding for all the mom's standing at the ice cream truck.

- Contact the local professional moving companies in your area and ask them to distribute new business packet info to their customers/clients to welcome them to their new home. Or ask about adding your business information to their "New Move" packets.

- Always be on the look out for new local businesses holding a grand opening event. Many times they are giving away freebies to the first few hundred customers plus you might get a mention in some promotions or ads.

- Inform your friends, family & co-workers that you offer freebies for any types of parties with more than ten people in attendance. Seek out those people who are holding baby showers, bridal showers, birthday parties, anniversary parties etc. and offer freebies for the goodie bags.

- Print out your own re-ordering labels if you sell consumable goods (foods, spices, soaps, bath products, cosmetics, etc.) make sure you stick on a small re-ordering info sticker with your business info on it so that your customer can easily locate your information for placing reorders. This is also important to do considering some customers purchase items from you to give as a gift, this way the person who received the gift will also know how to contact you and will become a potential new customer for you.

- Establish a referral tell-a-friend program for your business and print out referral coupons. Offer established customers a free little gift or personal discount if they refer a new customer to you.

- Print out Coloring Pages with a small section on them advertising your business and donate them to local area restaurants, schools, daycares etc.

  Try to find a design that relates to your business for the best effect.

- Contact your local area Girl Scouts, 4-H Club and other youth groups and talk to them about a project with the youth in the group. This is a great opportunity if you company offers a fundraiser program.

For Example: If you are a Kitchen Consultant, come in and teach the youth how to cook or about kitchen safety. If you sell pet products, go in and talk about grooming a pet. If you sell candles, go in and make some mini candles or teach them how to decorate them for gifts. Be creative!

- Make sure you leave information about your business on your answering machine or voice mail message. Not everyone who phones you knows that you sell or represent a particular company.

- Take your outdated catalogs and randomly mail or distribute them in your neighborhood. Make sure you stamp it OUTDATED/ for informational purposes only, then provide contact info so they can contact you if interested to get a current catalog.

- Get business themed banking checks. Your bank checks pass thru tons of hands that could become potential customers or party hosts. If possible get your email address or website URL preprinted on them as well.

- Research local children's Christmas party, Easter egg hunt, Halloween party, and get involved on the planning committees! You can donate candy or other holiday items and get yourself some business exposure for FREE.

- Contact local small shops in your area. Offer to sponsor a drawing box & prize. Make sure you have an attractive drawing box and have the prize on display. A lot of small shops have (in-store) drawings sponsored by other local merchants. You should also have on hand a few catalogs and a stack of business cards. This is a great way to get business exposure and to collect leads.

Make sure your entry form collects Name, phone number and email address Include a section to ask if they are interested in

_____ more info about hosting a party

_____ more info about a consultant opportunity

_____ request a free catalog

_____ subscribe to the online newsletter

- If you get magazines mailed to your home, after reading them, cover the current address label and print out new labels that read "Compliments of _____" and donate them to local doctors offices, dentist offices, local hospitals, libraries, community centers, senior centers, etc. Make sure your label includes your business name and contact information.

- Draft various mini tip booklets, recipe booklets or craft project booklets. Label the booklets "Courtesy of _____" and donate them to local daycare centers, salons, civic and community groups, etc.

- If your company has a fundraising in place, seek out local groups who are holding fundraisers so you can offer your catalog as their next fundraiser.

- Work with your local area Home Owners Association to research ways you can work together to promote your business. Perhaps offer a raffle drawing or free samples to go in the next mailing that is sent out to all homeowners.

- Get in touch with your local taxicab company donate catalogs and samples to place in the back seats of taxis. Bus companies, shuttle busses, airplanes and trains are also a great place to leave material as people are always looking for something to read in these environments.

- When you travel take numerous catalogs, flyers, business cards etc. with you when you pack for your trip. Make up a separate tote bag just for these items. Leave you catalogs, flyers and business cards ever where you go while on your trip.

SECTION 3
BEHIND THE CURTAIN OF THE
SUCCESSFUL NETWORK MARKETER

CHAPTER TWELVE

WHY SOME DON'T MAKE IT THE FIRST 90 DAYS

Yet another thing that all our successful Network Marketers have in common is each and every one of them have seen people come and go. The opportunities were exactly the same as were the products. The only difference was the dedication, drive and determination of the people who stayed and the people who were gone within the first 90, 60, 30 or sometimes even 15 days!

As a Network Marketer in a new industry, with a new company, in the business of introducing a new product to family, friends, aquaninences and strangers, a person would have to be a machine if there was not some hesitation and fear. Knowing this fact, the following is some advice from those expert panelists who have made it to the other side of the mountain and now have a very successful network marketing business.

1) The Law of Association is Real – Take a look at the attitudes and the bank accounts of the five people you spend the most time with and you will better understand why you are where you are. Knowing this, make a commitment to yourself that you will spend your time, both personally and professionally with positive and successful people, rather than negative and unsuccessful people. Limit the amount of interaction you have with "negative nellies" who might be looking to share their misery with you.

Secret Tip

Birds of a feather, flock together

2) Seek out leaders in your company, in your up line, or your peers and develop relationships with these winners. In advance, ask for the support of your spouse, partner, boyfriend, girlfriend, friends, parents or any single person who can give you support and encouragement. Do not sink into the negativity of small-minded people who are not running a successful network marketing business like you intend to do. Also, be certain that you are strengthening your mind set to be a positive thinking person who is driven and determined to succeed.

The Universe will in fact return exactly what you are thinking and acting upon.

3) If you become a rock star Network Marketing business owner, you will be earning more than the average lawyer. If you were a lawyer and you decided once you finished law school, to never again study case law or do research on new cases or rulings, you would become ignorant in your field in a very short amount of time. Likewise, if you do not make it a priority to learn more about your company, your products, your competition, sales techniques, business strategy and overall personal and professional development, you will find yourself sinking in the quicksand of incompetence.

4) You must make a concerted effort to be disciplined to seek knowledge continually. If you spend just a little time each day listening to or reading about sales strategy, the competition, etc. you will be well on your way to developing a six figure a year mindset that will lead you to fulfillment of all your personal and professional goals. The choice is yours to make it out of the first 90 days.

CHAPTER THIRTEEN

CHARACTERISTICS OF SUCCESSFUL PEOPLE

1) Have a sense of gratitude

2) Give other people credit for victories

3) Read everyday

4) Talk about ideas

5) Share information and ideas

6) Exude joy

7) Embrace change

8) Keep a to do project list

9) Compliment

10) Forgive others

11) Accept responsibilities for their failures

12) Keep a journal

13) Want others to succeed

14) Keep a to be list

15) Set goals and develop life plans

16) Continues learns

17) Operates from a transformational perspective

18) Organized

19) Has a dedicated work space and a routine

20) Self Control

21) Goes to Bed and gets plenty of sleep

22) Get serious about your health and wellness.

Characteristics of Unsuccessful People

1) Have a sense of entitlement

2) Takes all the credit for their victories

3) Watch TV everyday

4) Talk about people

5) Hordes information and data

6) Exude anger

7) Fear change

8) Fly by the seat of their pants

9) Criticizes

10) Holds a grudge

11) Blame others for their failures

12) Say they keep a journal but really don't

13) Secretly hope others fail

14) Don't know what they want to be

15) Never sets goals

16) Think they know it all

17) Operate from a transactional perspective

18) Disorganized

19) Does not have a dedicated work space

20) Finds delight in seeing others fail.

CHAPTER FOURTEEN

SERVANT LEADERSHIP

Another fiber that binds the successful network marketing panelists together is their focus on serving others. In serving others, they have all found a significant level of success that comes by not focusing on their own needs alone.

SECRET TIP

You can have anything you want in life if you focus on the needs of others, be it a customer or someone on your team, before you focus on your own needs and desires.

For some, being a servant leader has come naturally, for others; they pursued the servant leadership mindset.

There are many books, resources and training courses that teach what servant leadership is all about. Taking time to learn about servant leadership will be one of your most valued resources on your journey to success.

Can you find success without becoming a servant leader? Of course, but the goal of this chapter is about total fulfillment. The kind of fulfillment that comes through finding your own success along the path of serving others by helping them in any number of ways.

Spend time transforming your heart, head, hands and habits by exploring the teachings that come with being a servant leader and you will be on the path that can certainly change your life. We all have access to the greatest, most practical and effective leadership model that will benefit all situations – especially as you venture out on this new path to network marketing.

The Most Practical and Effective Leadership Model

No matter what your religious affiliation or belief in Jesus Christ as having walked this earth or if those stories are true fiction, one thing is certain, is that if you embrace the model of His leadership, that of a servant leader, it could possibly be the most life changing, transformational encounter you have ever experienced.

Business and leadership gurus, Ken Blanchard and Phil Hodges created an educational resource called Lead Like Jesus. If you choose to delve deeper into this or a similar resource, you will see that Jesus really did provide the most effective leadership model of our time. If you choose to learn and explore how to "Lead like Jesus" you will be on the path to becoming the ultimate Servant Leader. Jesus was very clear in that leadership was to be first and foremost an act of service. No plan B or alternative was even offered. Therefore, it is clear that servant leadership is in fact, a mandate.

The truly exciting part of this leadership model is that Jesus never sends us into any situation with a faulty plan or a plan to fail. When Jesus speaks on a subject, He guides us on a path that is in harmony with the Universe. When He speaks on leadership, He speaks to us on what is both right AND effective.

And how exciting for you that if you NEVER considered servant leadership as part of your path, the very fact you are reading this eBook about network marketing shows that again, you have put yourself in the right place at the right time. For while not mandated on the path to network marketing success, it is an important part of your success path, should you choose to make it as such.

So to better understand what a journey towards leading like Jesus looks like, lets focus on the two internal and two external domains that truly make up the DNA of a Servant Leader as outlined by Ken and Phil.

Internally – As a Servant Leader, you will start to give special attention to your heart and your head.

Externally – As a Servant Leader, you will start to give special attention to your hands and habits.

According to the Lead Like Jesus Leadership Model, when the heart, head, hands and habits are aligned in Servant Leadership, extraordinary levels of loyalty, trust and productivity will result. So let us dig in to these four domains a little deeper so you can best understand what it will take to transform your leadership model into that of a Servant Leader!

Servant Leadership is first a matter of your heart

When it comes to the heart, one of the first questions you need to ask yourself as a current or future leader is "Am I a servant leader or a self-serving leader?"

Key indicators of which you truly are can be found in the truthful answers to these questions:

1) How do you handle feedback?

2) How do you prepare your team for growth and succession planning?

3) How often do you ask your team to do something you are not willing to do?

4) Do you ever catch yourself taking credit, talking too much or showing off?

5) How often do you readily admit that you don't have all the answers?

Now be honest with your evaluation but don't be too hard on yourself either. If you find yourself falling short of the kind of leader you really want to be, make one of your daily goals to look closely at the motives of your heart. As Ken and Phil put it, "Every day we must recalibrate our heart." They go on to say to successfully combat temptations to be a self-serving leader; we need to daily surrender our motives and actions to Christ as our guide and role model for how we should lead.

Secret Tip

Imagine Who You Will Become When You Put Yourself Last.

The journey of life is to move from a self-serving heart to a serving heart. You finally become an adult when you realize life is about what you give instead of what you get. Now, if you have acknowledged some self-serving tendencies, be aware at the root are two causes: false pride and fear. So over the course of the next few days, take some time to identify your fears and sources of false pride. This will be a vital exercise to break negative impacts on both your personal and professional relationships and set you on course to becoming an effective servant leader.

If your goal is to be a true servant leader, your heart must undergo a complete and total transformation. You can NEVER again be who you are today.

Secret Tip

Trust in the Lord with all your HEART and lean not on your own understanding, In all your ways acknowledge Him and He shall direct your paths. Proverbs 3:5-6

Servant Leadership is a matter of your mind

If servant leadership starts in the heart with motivation and intent, the second internal domain, the mind, encompasses the leaders belief system and perspective on the role of a leader.

The reason a majority of corporations would never implement a servant leadership model is because they think there will be nothing but chaos with leaders trying to please everyone. The companies who think this way don't understand there are two organizational benefits to leadership that Jesus exemplified. As you launch your network marketing career and build you team, consider this:

Benefit #1 – Having a visionary role to always do the right thing

Benefit #2 – Having an implementation role of always doing things right

To be an effective servant leader at the top of your down line, you must have the ability to communicate effectively with your team the vision you set forth as a servant leader. As a servant leader, it will be your responsibility to inspire your teams, to set them on fire with your vision, leadership, training and beliefs.

Secret Tip

No team will grow and rise above the passion of its leadership

As a servant leader, the mission of the company you represent and the mission you have for your team needs to be ingrained at a cellular level. Your people must be on fire so they too forget about themselves and focus on the quality of life of their customers and the teams in their down line.

Key indicators to show if you are truly focusing on customers and your teams can be found in the truthful answers to these questions:

1) What is the WHY of each of your team members?

2) What are the goals and needs of the customers?

3) Do we know why are customers are interested in our product or why should they be?

4) What is the true benefit to recruiting a new team member or gaining a new customer?

Now maybe you don't know those answers yet and perhaps you thought of some other important questions you need answers to and that is a good sign that one of your personal goals in network marketing will be to become a servant leader. Because whether they know it or not, your teams will be looking to you to clarify, define, communicate and LIVE for something beyond just a paycheck. It will be your role as a servant leader to lead by example and set your teams on their own servant leadership path.

Secret Tip

If you are serious about Servant Leadership, just look at the ultimate example Jesus gave as a crystal clear vision when He got down on His hands and knees and washed the filthy feet of His disciples in John 13:1-17.

The master became the servant and His focus transitioned from visionary to implementation. And that is the foundation of Servant Leadership. It is about the effective implementation that turns the traditional "Boss/Manager" hierarchy on its head. You need your teams to see you acting and building something different. This will change the way they build and treat their teams and so on and so forth. Your entire down line needs to feel that what you are building is not about power and control. Rather it is about helping teams live and experience something completely different. Customers will feel the difference, by the way, and by focusing on their needs and benefits, more sales will untimely be the result.

As leaders, you will be measured by the success of the teams you develop. That is when true success will be yours.

Servant Leadership is a matter of your hands

To this point we have seen that the heart and the mind are two very important domains that dictate what kind of leader you will become. As we learned from Ken and Phil, who used Jesus as their Servant Leadership model, the heart encompasses the motivation and intent of a leader and the mind encompasses the belief system and perspective of a servant leader. Then the external domain begins with the hands, which encompasses the application of leadership behavior.

Secret Tip

The application of leadership behavior is a willingness to change to be a Servant Leader. It means actually changing your behavior and asking what Jesus would do BEFORE you act on a situation.

Effective servant leadership comes to life when the heart and the mind now guide the behavior in your interaction with your team, customers, community members and yes, even your family and friends. For you cannot be a servant leader in the professional area of your life, and not in the personal side of your life. This is not a behavior that can be compartmentalized.

It is when the hands start to bear good fruit through good intention and right thinking and right actions that you find yourself on the path to being a true Servant Leader. How then do you want your leadership remembered by the people on your team, in your home and your community? Because being a Servant Leader, in other words, Leading Like Jesus, is not just a website, or a book, or a workshop – nor is it a catch phrase. No, to lead like Jesus and become a true Servant Leader is a lifestyle! It is a total self-reconstruction making the development of our teams and the focus of the best interests of our customers as equally, if not MORE important, than personal success is the true choice of a Servant Leader.

To be a Servant Leader is following the business model of Jesus and pouring your life into the lives of others in a way that separates you from their interactions with others. They will feel the difference and be drawn to whatever it is in you that is different. What they are feeling and what they are drawn to is the genuine concern that you have for their wellbeing and success above your own! What they are feeling is your CHOICE to leave a legacy of service … to everyone with whom you interact on a daily, weekly, monthly and annual basis.

Servant Leadership is a Matter of Your Habits

Nothing in your heart, mind or hands will change if you do not pay special attention to your habits. To say it is last in order of the four domains would be a mistake for all are equally important and must be given equal attention. To work on only one would be going to a health club only to work out one of your limbs and let the other three remain unchanged.

Remember yesterday when you showered? Or maybe it was this morning? Maybe you showered just before downloading this eBook. Either way, just because you showered earlier does not mean you are clean forever. The shower you took today will not last more than 24 hours, maybe even less depending on what you have done since your last shower. The point is, the shower you took today will not last forever and you really must shower daily, at least.

That is the same with habits. What you focus on today must be focused again and again and again. Therefore habits really are the daily recalibration of your commitment to a vision. Before something truly becomes a habit, it must be practiced again and again and again as a discipline.

Habits of a Successful Servant Leader

As Jesus moved through His season of earthly leadership, He was under constant pressure and temptation to be drawn off course by the failings of His friends, His followers, His family and even His enemies. Through it all, Jesus modeled five key habits to stay on track with His mission, according to the Lead Like Jesus workbook.

These five habits were the primary antidote He applied to counter the opposing forces in His life, and as you can see, you can easily apply these to every opposing situation in your professional and personal life to stay on course to become a Servant Leader:

1) Solitude - If you have a need to always be around people, stop it. You must find time to be alone with your thoughts, to plan, to play, to pray.

2) Prayer / Mediate – Find time to talk to God about the little things and the big things.

3) Knowledge – you must learn more than what you know today. To be successful you must be on a never-ending quest for knowledge.

4)   Accept and Respond to God's unconditional love

5)   Maintain accountability. Always. The buck stops with you.

Tips to Change a Bad Habit or Create a Good Habit

Reading tips about how to change a habit won't do a single thing. But, it's a start. Do you bite your nails? Indulge in comfort food? Text and drive? Gossip? Smoke? Procrastinate? Regardless of your particular habit, or how deeply ingrained it is, the process of breaking it will be similar. With persistence and the right mindset, it's possible to break your bad habits, and these instructions help you through the process of doing so.

Commit to a goal. Although it may seem obvious, it is important to understand that the first step in breaking a bad habit developing a true desire for and commitment to changing your life. Many people embark on the path of breaking a habit without being certain that they really want to change. Breaking habits is a difficult task, so if you aren't fully committed to it you are likely to fail.

Understand your habit. Most habitual behaviors are patterns that have evolved because they have been rewarded in some way. They make it easier to perform a common task, or to deal with various emotional states, resulting in a "reward" in the form of neurochemicals that trigger our brains' pleasure centers. Many bad habits come about as a means of dealing with situations that cause stress or boredom.

Make a plan. Once you understand the situation that triggers your habit and the reward you receive for engaging in the undesirable behavior, you can make a plan that involves goals for behavior change and strategies for minimizing habit triggers. Plan to make mistakes. Do not make a plan that will be deemed a failure as a result of a single slip-up.

Visualize success. In your mind, repeatedly practice breaking the habit by imagining scenarios in which you engage in desired behaviors rather than the bad habit. Imagine situations in which you would be tempted to engage in the undesired behavior and choose a better option. This helps reinforce positive behavior patterns.

For example, if your goal is to eat less junk food, imagining yourself in your kitchen preparing a healthy meal, and sitting down to eat it. Some people find it helpful to write down "scripts" of their desired behavior and read them every day.

Practice awareness. Be conscious of when you are tempted to give in to bad habits. What are the situations that lead to the undesired behavior? What are the sensations in your body or thoughts in your mind that promote the undesired behavior? Understanding them without judging yourself will help you resist.

Don't suppress thoughts about the habit. If you try not thinking about something, ironically, you will start to see it everywhere and become overwhelmed. Trying not to think about smoking, for example, will only lead you to hypersensitive to anything that reminds you of smoking. You are much better off to recognize your craving and the situations that promote it, and deal with these issues head-on.

Habits

Adopting new and changing old habits is essential to becoming a Servant Leader. Of course this effort will not flow effortlessly at first but eventually they can and will become a core element of your very being. So do not give up when there is a set back. Discipline yourself to practice daily and before you know it, they will be habits that transformed you from the inside out.

CHAPTER FIFTEEN

HANDLING REJECTION

Thick skin. If you are easily offended, embarrassed or take everything personally, you have two choices:

1) Realize that Network Marketing is NOT for you

2) Change those behaviors because none are healthy or helpful.

Secret Tip

Success Will Be Found OUTSIDE of Your Comfort Zone.

Since you are still reading, you have chosen choice number 2! Good for you. Now, the first thing we want to cover the need for you to learn the difference between REJECTION or an OBJECTION. Knowing the difference will be very important to both your mental health and your paycheck.

Is it Rejection or is it an Objection?

To understand the difference between REJECTION and OBJECTION, first let us look at the foundation for overcoming an objection. By combining many of the methods of our expert panelists, you might find the following S.A.A.S.S system to be a very useful strategy to overcome objections or responding to prospect concerns

Counter objections using S.A.A.S.S

STOP:

- Stop and listen. Think about what the prospect has just said to you. Nod your head so they get the non-verbal cue that you are listening and seeking understanding.

- Make it very clear that you have stopped your sales presentation and you are listening to their objection or concern.

- Make certain that your response is well thought out and personalized for them so they do not feel as if you are just continuing with your sales pitch.

  o It is very important they feel that you are actually responding to their specific objection and not just repeating a prepared response, or worse than that, just bulldozing over and ignoring their objection.

AGREE:

- Agree that the concern or some part of it is valid (or would be if the prospect had all the information about your product or was thinking about his/her needs or goals more realistically.)

- Agreement helps avoid debate so coming up with some sort of agreement point will take the prospects guard down. Their natural hesitation to buy something new will be softened now that you have not tried to prove them wrong by pushing back with your scripted facts.

Example: I agree that you do not want to spend your hard earned money on a product that will not help you meet your health and wellness goals.

ASK A QUESTION:

- After an objection, that you seemingly agreed with, it is important to get to the bottom of the real objection so you can better understand the prospects concern.

- Asking a question also shows that you listened and you are interested in what the prospect had to say.

- It is also an opportunity to learn more about the prospect so you can ensure you are fitting the proper product(s) with the needs and goals of the prospect.

- Asking a question opens up a dialogue – usually friendly – rather that pushing back to show the prospect why they are wrong in their objection.

- Asking a question shows confidence and belief in your products and company, while showing humility.

SHARE A SUCCESS STORY:

- You are going to have plenty of examples of how well your products worked either from your own personal experience, or your up line or your current customers.

- Sharing these success stories in response to an objection is yet another way a prospect can agree with you without making it seem like they lost an argument or making it seem like their objection was wrong.

- Sharing success stories takes you out of the equation as a sales person and instead highlights the success others have had with the product(s)

- A short success story makes you a teacher rather than an adversarial sales person. (Many of the successful panelists testified they are in the role of teacher and trainer or even life coach, rather than sales person)

SUGGEST A PRODUCT:

- At this point, after you have listened, agreed, ask a question, shared a success story, the prospect wants to buy from you.

- Making a suggestion about what product(s) will help them meet a specific need or personal goal will enable you to get the sale without the prospect actually having to say the word YES.

- Even if the prospect does not like the specific product suggestion you have made, it opens up the conversation to introduce other product offerings that will be in line with their specific needs and goals.

There is no limit to the amount of times you can use SAASS in one conversation. As long as the prospect is throwing up more objections, you can begin the entire system over again.

When a No is Really a No

There will be times in your career that you will get through your entire presentation, share all the benefits, discuss the prospects goals, needs... and you will still get a NO. So what! Move on. There are unlimited amounts of people out there who need what you have!

Rejected!

Let's be honest — you are not going to get a YES from every prospect. In fact, in order to be a successful network marketer, you are going to get more NO's than YES's simply because any type of sales is a true numbers game. That means you must get a certain number of NO's in order to get a certain number of YES's.

SECRET TIP

Be excited about each and every NO you get because

that means you are one NO closer to your next YES!

You are going to have to put your NO's into perspective. Closing sales means you will hear NO. And you will hear it A LOT! It just is not possible to be in network marketing without facing this fact: You will hear NO three times more than you hear YES. One of the differentiating factors that will make you more successful than other network marketers is that you will get an answer, even if it is a NO. Mediocre network marketers avoid getting an answer. They fear hearing NO. If you promote your product with fear of hearing NO, that means you are going to hear YES a lot less.

You have to remember that in this world, your time really is money so you cannot waste it on getting sucked into the MAYBE vortex. Finally getting a solid answer from someone is a great feat because that means you can mark that particular prospect off your follow-up list and move on to someone else. Remember, you are representing a great company with great products, so there are plenty of people out there who NEED and WANT what you are offering.

You will become a very successful network marketer when you learn and live in a world where you earn an informed NO from prospects who truly are not interested in your product offerings.

CHAPTER SIXTEEN

THE MINDSET OF A WINNER

To succeed in Network Marketing and in life, you must believe that you are a winner. Did you know you will never rise above your own self-image? That means the only person limiting how far you can go and how great you can become is ... well, YOU!

Self-Discipline

Launching your Network Marketing business will be one of the most exciting, hopeful and stressful times of your life. The buck stops with you and you hold the keys to your success ... or your failure. There will be no manager or boss breathing down your neck or micro-managing your every move. You must learn to self-manage and become disciplined in the following characteristics:

1)   **Emotionally Stable** – Network Marketers who self-manage are emotionally stable. You must understand the value of

the product(s) you are selling and you must understand the value of the Network Marketing business model on a very basic level. Your belief bank must be filled so you can remain certain in tough selling situations because daily your motives, products and company will be called into question. On those tough days, as an emotionally stable network marketers you must not be too hard on yourself yet on good days, you can't get too high on the success that you blow off the basics of what you need to accomplish for the day. Successful Network Marketers who are emotionally stable do not have to continually be talking on their cell phones to others complaining about how busy they are or how tough of a day it has been. As an emotionally stable Network Marketer, you must have a significant reserve of personal strength and self-discipline.

2) **Extremely Active and Informed** - Network Marketers who self manage are very active in their business and are very informed about all aspects of their business. As a successful Network Marketing professional, your professional and personal life will not be separate. You will have to seek out every opportunity to let people know what you do and why you do it. You must be informed about the company

that you represent, the products you sell and the numbers you need to hit to be successful. Time must be placed into evaluating what is working and what is not working. Daily and weekly review must take place so you can figure out what you are doing right, and where you need improvement. You are going to track and monitor your personal success as well as your team. You are going to actively set optimistic and realistic goals based on very strategic planning. Your up line management will not have a question for you that you haven't already asked yourself in your strategic planning. Being active, informed, organized and on top of your numbers are all characteristics in the mindset of a winner.

3) **Proactive Planning** – Network Marketers who self manage will always be thinking ahead and will always be planning proactively. Every day, every social event, every vacation, every dinner out is an opportunity to network and meet new people who will need what you have to offer. Remember, you are representing a great company and you are passionate about the products you offer. Your products have an important benefit to your customer's lives, so therefore you must always be proactively planning and prospecting.

There is a common theme that runs between all of the experts we interviewed for this eBook. If you are serious about Network Marketing, you will want to begin to weave these traits into the fiber of your being. It will not happen overnight, but if you are disciplined and deliberate about this opportunity, you cannot stay where you are today.

Mental Toughness

The mindset of a winning Network Marketer includes inner strength and a mental toughness that the average person does not possess. The strongest Network Marketers believe that nothing is impossible and nothing is beyond reach. You must learn to thrive on the challenge and put all obstacles into perspective as an opportunity.

Network Marketing is not a get rich quick scheme, in fact the successful Network Marketers love what they do and they typically don't consider it work. Therefore, the hours they put in, while lengthy, are not painful but rather it is fun! You will need to recondition your attitude and your mental disposition to work hard and work long. As we have mentioned, sales success in Network Marketing is numbers game. The more prospects you see, the more products you will sell and the more team you will recruit into your down line.

The Mindset of a Winner

Do not squander this opportunity. What you are seeking in life is found in the opportunity that Network Marketing holds.

You were born to win. But to be a winner, you must plan to win, prepare to win, and expect to win.

You are the next great Network Marketing success story. Go forth and do amazing things!

ADDENDUM – EXPERT PANEL OF NETWORK MARKETERS

1) Jeannine Quigley

   Arbonne Consultant

   219.775.5356

   jmquigley.myarbonne.com

2) Nicole Breger

   Herbalife Consultant

   219-793-3294

   nicole.breger.16@facebook.com

3) Summer Davis

   Young Living Consultant

   708-220-1410

   svandeventer@msn.com

4) Alan Jones

   Nerium Consultant

   502-593-4977

Aljon76@aol.com

Alanjones123.nerium.com

5) Kyle Hooker
Origami Owl Consultant
219-613-7236
kyleloveslockets@gmail.com

kylehooker.origamiowl.com

6) Elizabeth Hough
Mary Kay Consultant
219-246-6142
ehough@marykay.com

www.marykay.com/ehough

7) Jeremy Bowen
Avocare Consultant
312-768-9291
jbwen@gmail.com

8) Nicole Breger
Seacret Skin Care Consultant
219-793-3294

9) Jenni Walters

   Rodan + Fields Consultant

   jenniwalters.myrandf.com

   jenniwalters.myrandf.biz (for business)

10) Beverly Boner

   Pampered Chef Consultant

   219-239-3555

   https://www.facebook.com/beverly.boner

CONCLUSION

Thank you again for downloading this book!

If you enjoyed this book, then I'd like to ask you for a favor, would you be kind enough to leave a review for this book on Amazon? It'd be greatly appreciated!

Help us better serve you by sending questions or comments to greatreadspublishing@gmail.com - Thank you!

The Course that Had the Most Impact in Our Business...

15 people per week into your NETwork marketing business.

I thought you might be interested in this "explosive" training course. Steve Smith is a 20 year veteran of the NETwork marketing Industry and also a dear friend of ours.

Click Here...

He has put together without doubt the most in-depth coaching course how to build your NETwork Marketing team just using the Internet. His coaching course "Bringing the NET into NETwork Marketing" is proving be the most sort after in the field of NETwork marketing.

Check out this link and see for your self. He also offers you a 60 day no quibble money back guarantee, that is how confident he is you will enjoy and benefit from his in-depth training modules.

60 modules covering EVERY aspect on building your NETwork marketing business using the POWER of the Internet. It's a Step by Step system that allows you to earn while you learn.

No Risk 60 Guarantee - Lets do it - Click here!

My hope is you fully invest 100% into the course! Email and let me know how it goes.

See you at the top,

Kelly Cruze

Made in the USA
Lexington, KY
12 May 2015